THE DISFLUENT
CHILD

THE DISFLUENT CHILD
A Management Program

by
Daniel H. Zwitman, Ph.D.
Director, Speech Clinic
and
Assistant Professor, Head and Neck Surgery
UCLA School of Medicine

UNIVERSITY PARK PRESS
Baltimore

WM
475
Z98d
1978

UNIVERSITY PARK PRESS
International Publishers in Science and Medicine
233 East Redwood Street
Baltimore, Maryland 21202

Typeset by Everybodys Press.
Manufactured in the United States of America
by The Maple Press Company.

Library of Congress Cataloging in Publication Data

Zwitman, Daniel H., 1943-
The disfluent child.

Includes bibliographical references.
1. Speech disorders in children—Psychological aspects. 2. Parent and
child. I. Title. [DNLM: 1. Speech disorders—Therapy. 2. Speech
disorders—In infancy & childhood. WM475.3 Z98d]
RJ496.S7Z84   618.9'28'554   78-6163
ISBN 0-8391-1277-7

Contents

	Preface	vii
CHAPTER 1	Rationale for Counseling Parents of the Disfluent Child...................	1
CHAPTER 2	Evaluation of the Disfluent Child	7
	Disfluency	8
	The Evaluation Procedure	11
	Pre/Post Program Rating Scale	14
CHAPTER 3	Treatment of Abnormal and Normal Disfluency: A Child Management Program	15
	Development and Testing of the Child Management Program	17
	Purpose of the Program	19
	Administering the Program	20
	Program Sections......................	21
	Selecting Appropriate Program Sections .	21
	Schedule for Program Administration	23
	Questionnaires and Checklists	24
CHAPTER 4	Child Management Program	27
SECTION I	How to Deal with Your Child's Speech	29
	Questionnaire	32
	Checklist	33
SECTION II	How to Deal With Your Child's Speech (continued)............................	35
	Questionnaire	37
	Checklist	38
SECTION III	How to Improve Self-Concept and Security ...	39
	Questionnaire	42
	Checklist	43
SECTION IV	How to React When Your Child Unintentionally Misbehaves	45

                        Questionnaire 47
                        Checklist 48

SECTION V   How to React When Your Child
                        Intentionally Misbehaves 49
                        Questionnaire 52
                        Checklist 55

SECTION VI   Responding Consistently to Your Child's
                        Misbehaviors 57
                        Questionnaire 59
                        Checklist 60

SECTION VII   Constructing a Star Chart 61
                        Questionnaire 67
                        Checklist 68

APPENDIX I   Pre/Post Program Rating Scale 71

APPENDIX II   Questionnaire Answers 75

                        Literature Cited 79

Preface

This program is designed to guide the clinician in counseling parents and family concerned about their disfluent child. The author has frequently observed the questioning, guilt-ridden look on parents' faces when they find themselves confronted with an eruption in their child's communication. They may have tried to follow advice to ignore the disfluencies, or they may have attempted to keep their child content while fruitlessly searching for the cause of the problems with his speech. Furthermore, they may point to another family known to them to be in a constant state of turmoil but having children who are fluent; they ask why in their own relatively stable home they have a child who "stutters." "Wait and see" advice worries them, and they come to the clinician for answers.

This program incorporates many of the recommendations found in the speech and behavioral psychology literature and the author's own clinical experience, but the program is not presented as the ultimate treatment for what has been termed abnormal disfluency, early stuttering, or childhood stuttering. Its purpose is to provide the disfluent child with a loving, fair, and consistent home that exerts minimal communicative stress. In the process, it should reduce parental concern about the child's speech.

As with any tool, the success of this program will depend upon the qualifications and experience of the clinician who uses it. The program was administered and modified continually and should be a detailed, self-explanatory guide for the counseling regimen. However, the important "individuality" of therapy will have to be provided by the clinician's careful emphasis on those principles most pertinent to his client's particular situation.

I would like to gratefully acknowledge the dedicated assistance of Judith Sonderman, who helped me with the initial draft and three years of development and who lent her expertise to the final preparation of the manuscript. I am also indebted to Drs. Hugo Gregory, Richard Schiefelbusch, Charles Van Riper, and Jack Wetter for their editorial commentary. Lastly, I thank Christine Allan, who typed and retyped the text.

THE DISFLUENT CHILD

CHAPTER 1

Rationale for Counseling Parents of the Disfluent Child

Between two-and-a-half and six years of age a child moves through a rapid phase of speech expansion and acquires numerous language transformations that meet the demands of his increasingly complex environment. He finds he must interact verbally with others in order to obtain what he desires, and he realizes that his brothers and sisters and other children are often competing for the same items. At some point he probably determines that the quality of his speech or the dexterity with which he presents his case may be directly related to the acquisition of his needs. Therefore, the child faces two major hurdles: first, to develop an intact communicative system, and, second, to successfully employ that system in his environment.

As adults we value articulate and fluent speech. We judge others by the skill and ease with which they communicate, because we are impressed not only by what a person says, but also by how well he says it. For example, we are aware of the vocabulary he uses, his delivery, his accent, his articulation, his voice quality, his speaking rate, and the way in which he sequences his words.

Parents admire the same verbal dexterity demonstrated in a child. They may actually be more responsive to the child who can communicate proficiently than they are to the one who has difficulty meeting adult standards of speech. It is this underlying criterion of "good" speech that may subtly result in environmental pressure for fluency. If older siblings are present, they may set a communication standard that evokes a more favorable response from their parents than the belabored and simplistic speech of the younger child. Therefore, the child may try to reach for this inherent speech level before he is ready to do so.

Not only may a child feel he needs to communicate more proficiently, he may also have time pressures while he is conversing. An adult speaks rapidly, usually knows what he wants to say, and has at his command the words needed to communicate the message. In fact, adults usually are very intolerant of time delays and quickly fill in if the other person has difficulty expressing himself. A child may feel that he will not have enough time to speak, or at least may be concerned that he will lose his parents' attention or his turn if he delays. Therefore, in most family situations the child tries to develop a complex communication system, but he may face environmental factors that make this difficult.

We know that the dexterity to master speech and language varies among children. Some children will be delayed in their acquisition of semantics, syntax, or pragmatics, others will be inarticulate, and still others will stutter. Although a well-defined etiology can be isolated for some speech and language disorders, the cause (or causes) for stuttering remains obscure. There is, however, some indication that early stuttering may be associated with retarded speech development. Van Riper (1971) found that, of 44 early stutterers, approximately 20 percent failed to use phrases or sentences until three to six years of age, and the onset of stuttering coincided with the production of connected speech. This information entertains the hypothesis that other children who acquire intact speech and language may still be susceptible to motoric dysfunction (stuttering). That is, the normal disfluencies heard in all childrens' speech as they are mastering language may increase in severity in those children who have developed connected language but who are still struggling to stabilize the neurological process of speaking. The hesitations they experience, which seem to overcome the child and to be out of control, and which momentarily prevent continuation, may signal a breakdown in the communicative system. Because in many cases stuttering recovery occurs as a function of age (Wingate, 1976), longitudinal improvement may result from maturation of motoric function.

As aptitude is a variance, so is environmental stress and the psychological ramifications it elicits. Negative emotions created by environmental factors may tax a less than stabilized communicative system and abnormal disfluencies may result. Therefore, another hypothesis may be proposed concerning environmental pressure and speech: It is usually easier for a child to communicate when environmental pressure, social disapproval, or communicative stress are minimal than it is when they occur frequently. Considerable support for this hypothesis can be found in the literature. Davis (1939), Johnson (1942, 1949), and Bloodstein (1975) attributed a child's abnormal disfluency to the over-critical attitude of his parents. Van Riper (1963, 1973) suggested that parents be attentive listeners and avoid situations where the child competed for the floor or communicated with the fear of interruption. Learning theorists also indict environmental factors in the onset of stuttering. Brutten and Shoemaker (1967) related fluency failure to cognitive and motor disorganization resulting from "negative emotion." This emotion was evoked by aversive stimuli in the child's environment. Shames and Sherrick (1963) felt that the parents could shape normal disfluencies into stuttering by first reinforcing, then punishing, their occurrence.

Although the relationship between environmental factors and abnormal disfluency has been well supported in the literature, there is a lack of data-based evidence. Information is available from behavior therapists concerning the modification of adult stuttering (Gray and England, 1969; Shames and Egolf, 1976), but learning models have been applied only in general terms in discussions of the disfluent child. Therefore, we do not have data that demonstrate which environmental factors are aversive to speech, or, if they are identified, which children are the most susceptible to these noxious stimuli. Asking recovered stutterers about positive and negative environmental factors (Johnson, 1951; Wingate, 1976) tends to cloud the issue because the vagueness of the retrospective interview leads to generalities. Therefore, it is not surprising to find that recovered stutterers report their homes were not conducive to fluency because of continual arguing, tension, and strict parents, but these same factors are common to many homes where fluency is not a problem. Some recovered stutterers report that their parents helped them with their speech while others say they did not. Frequently, their parents told them to "slow down" or "speak slowly" and reportedly this was of significant benefit. Since most authorities believe that telling a child to "slow down" is detrimental to fluency, the contradiction is apparent. However, reliable data, in addition to these subjective impressions, are necessary. If further research reveals that telling a child to "slow down" does improve his fluency, there is still the need to explore and isolate the numerous other environmental factors that may affect his speech.

In the final analysis, if environmental factors appear to cause or at least increase the severity of stuttering, as the widespread support for this theory indicates, then a plan of therapeutic intervention might be formulated upon this theory until research proves otherwise. However, such intervention strategies are not clearly outlined in the literature. Traditionally, the clinician has been instructed to advise parents to reduce the stressful conditions that appear to precipitate abnormal disfluency. Parents are to be counseled not to call their child's attention to his disfluency, to be responsive listeners, and to avoid interruptions, competition for the floor, time pressures, and other fluency disruptors. As pertinent as these suggestions may be, generally the literature fails to define the regimen for providing this counseling. Therefore, a systematic counseling program is necessary. Johnson (1959) concluded that parent counseling was an effective way to reduce stuttering, but his description of the method employed raises questions about its thoroughness. He describes the program as "that which could be done in the limited time available during the one day devoted in each case to the interview."

It is interesting that with all the volumes published in the field of stuttering, a minimal amount of research has focused specifically on the treatment of the early stutterer. Johnson's 1949 work, "An Open Letter to the Mother of a Stuttering Child" continues to be the cornerstone for much of the advice the clinician provides to parents. Although it is an excellent paper, this author doubts that Johnson intended that clinicians would use it so exclusively without regard to the complex process of guiding and changing parental behavior.

Counseling parents is an intricate process for two reasons. First, general advice provided orally, or in letter form, followed by general questions that examine its success, is often prone to counseling failure. Too much information too soon can overwhelm a parent. Advice apparently needs to be provided slowly and methodically, with periodic follow-up, in order to ensure that the parents incorporate the suggestions provided. Second, parent counseling often cannot be limited to only the parents' reaction to a child's disfluency; it must also involve their entire interrelationship with the child. We may feel we have been successful in counseling if a mother reports that she no longer interrupts her child when he is talking, but what if she is loving and understanding one day when he misbehaves, then spanks him the next day for the same action? As Glasner (1947) noted, "A calm and consistent household is far less likely to produce stuttering than a household where the atmosphere is indecisive and capricious."

In conclusion, two hypotheses have been developed from the information and data available on the etiology of early stuttering and its treatment. The parent counseling program outlined in this manuscript is based upon these hypotheses. To review, a child must develop a complex communicative system between the ages of two and six years of age. Disfluency, especially early stuttering, may result from a child's failure to stabilize his communicative system so that it functions adequately under communicative stress. Because early stuttering has a tendency to dissipate with age (maturation), therapeutic intervention should be directed towards providing a child with as conducive an environment for fluency as possible until the time he stabilizes his communicative system.

CHAPTER 2

Evaluation of the Disfluent Child

Any treatment program is predicated on a thorough diagnostic and evaluative procedure. The format of the initial interview and the decision to recommend the program in this text for a particular patient will likely be influenced by the clinician's theoretical viewpoint and experience. Nevertheless, the constant purpose of an evaluation is to obtain information necessary to formulate beneficial recommendations. This requires assessment of the child's normal or abnormal speech pattern and exploration of his home environment, especially the parent/child relationship. It is not the purpose of this text to outline a method for analysis of disfluency or to prepare the clinician to scrutinize a child's environment; rather, specific information on disfluency and the parent interview is provided that might assist the clinician with the evaluation. The characteristics that distinguish normal disfluency from what has been termed abnormal disfluency, early stuttering, or childhood stuttering are reviewed in the next section, but only as a guide, because a differential diagnosis must be based on the clinician's own system. The parent interview focuses on the parents' perception of the child's disfluency during the time they observe him with the clinician and at home. Circumstances surrounding the onset of the problem should be explored in conjunction with present environmental factors. Early stuttering may start dramatically, and, in some cases, a specific incident, such as a new teacher, a different child care center, or difficulty separating from the parents at nursery school, may result in an increase in disfluency. In other cases, an emotional upheaval in the family may trigger a sudden onset of stuttering. Psychological referral may be necessary, especially if the condition appears continual and not easily alleviated. In most cases, isolated causative factors will not be apparent, and the clinician must then decide if general child management information is appropriate or if the home situation is so troubled that referral to a child psychologist or psychiatrist is warranted. Parents who report that they constantly fight with each other and their children, or parents who say that their child is "out of control" to a degree that they cannot tolerate, probably need the guidance of a psychiatrist or psychologist.

Most family situations are not in a crisis state. In fact, even after an extensive interview it is frequently hard to identify unusually deviant circumstances. However, the general environments of many children without speech problems are filled with pressures, inconsistencies, and unfair treatment that they must endure. These negative factors may also be present in the everyday routine of the child who is susceptible to disfluent speech. They may affect his ability to acquire or maintain fluency. The clinician may help the parents eliminate these pressures and inconsistencies in their child's environment by providing them with concise guidelines for responding to the disfluencies, managing the child's misbehaviors, and rewarding him for appropriate behavior. If the clinician feels that he or she has the background and experience necessary to counsel parents concerned about their disfluent child, then the program outlined in this text can serve as a detailed format. The author has no way of judging each clinician's expertise, but it is hoped that those who use this program will carefully review, study, and scrutinize the contents before implementing it.

DISFLUENCY

In order to treat the child who is disfluent, the characteristics of disfluency, its description and progression, need to be understood, and those events that appear to either increase or decrease its occurrence need to be identified. Disfluency is the opposite of fluency, which is defined as the ability to produce the motor sequences in speech effortlessly, smoothly, and rapidly. If a child repeats, hesitates, and prolongs with greater frequency and effort than most children, he is stuttering (abnormally disfluent).

In early childhood, the demarcation between normal and abnormal disfluency may not be definitive, since all children are disfluent. Davis (1939, 1940) found that repetitions were part of the speech of all children, and Johnson (1942, 1959) emphasized that what might be perceived by the listener as stuttering was probably normal nonfluency that could be identified in every child's speech. However, even these authors found evidence that some children presented speech patterns unlike those of the rest. Davis concluded that the instance and number of syllable repetitions did distinguish those children who deviated markedly from others. Johnson found that the group identified as stutterers had significantly more prolongations. Studies by Egland (1955), Johnson (1959), Young (1961), Van Riper (1971), and Wingate (1976) revealed that listeners used the following features, particularly a and b, to distinguish stuttering from normal disfluency:

a. *Two or more repetitions* of a syllable or sound in three or more words per one hundred.

   Example 1: "See-see-see the bird!" as distinguished from "See-see the bird!" the latter of which may not be stuttering depending upon the effort involved.

   Example 2: "Ti-ti-tiger," as distinguished from "ti-tiger," which is uncertain and "tiger, tiger," which is probably normal.

   Example 3: "G-g-get the bird!" as differentiated from "G-get the bird!" which is questionable.

b. *Voiced prolongations* longer than one second and more than one per hundred words (usually visual and auditory cues reveal effort), or *silent prolongations* (hesitations or blocks) with inappropriate oral or facial movements occurring before a familiar word rather than before one requiring thought.

c. *Interjections* characterized by several repetitions of "uh," as distinguished from a normal extraneous utterance (i.e., "uh," "um," "well").

d. *Additional characteristics* that may be present: facial grimace, eye blinking, lips pressed tightly, mouth open, and breath holding.

Based upon the information presented in the literature, one can conclude that there are clear distinctions between normal and abnormal disfluency. However, this conclusion entertains the question of whether or not there is a progressive relationship between the two. The concept of progression, i.e., stuttering develops progressively from normal disfluency, probably received its major impetus from Bluemel (1932), who distinguished between "primary" and "secondary" stuttering, and from Johnson

(1942), who found that most children diagnosed as stutterers were actually normally nonfluent, but even those children who demonstrated hypertonic repetitions, prolongations, or conspicuous pauses were probably initially nonfluent before they were diagnosed as stutterers by their parents. Shames and Sherrick (1963), using an operant model, also hypothesized that stuttering began as normal disfluencies that were initially and differentially reinforced. As the child's speech became increasingly and noticeably disfluent, social, parental, or self disapproval was evoked, and the child's struggle with disfluencies led to stuttering.

Although these theories are well presented, there is little longitudinal data that actually demonstrate the developmental course of stuttering. Bloodstein (1960) compared different age groups between two and sixteen years, and concluded that if stuttering continued, it became more severe with increasing age. Easy repetitions and fluent periods diminished, while hard contacts and avoidance reactions increased. On the basis of these data, he divided stuttering into four phases. Van Riper (1963) also discussed primary, transitional, and secondary stuttering, but in a more recent work (1971) he revoked the concept of phases and stages and maintained that until adequate longitudinal data are available, this concept should be discarded. Instead, treatment should fit a child's needs as they are demonstrated by his current speech behavior, and therapy should not be prescribed according to a developmental category. Wingate (1976) also noted the lack of valid data to support the progression concept of stuttering, and he recommended that emphasis should be placed on direct and verifiable observations and individual consideration of the particular features of each case.

If a distinction can be made between normal and abnormal disfluency, then normally and abnormally disfluent children should be distinguishable in the clinic. Children who are normally disfluent communicate freely and are unaware of their disfluencies, as are most of the people who listen to them. Their disfluencies consist primarily of even, effortless repetitions. The problem is clearly in the way the parents listen to their child's speech. They may be very concerned parents who are overreacting to slight hesitations or repetitions. When the clinician listens to the normally disfluent child, it is apparent to him that the youngster is communicating easily, albeit with infrequent and non-interfering disfluencies.

Conversely, the child who displays a distinctive disfluency that clearly interrupts the flow of speaking and even interferes with his ability to communicate is abnormally disfluent. Frequent occurrences of repetitions and prolongations may characterize his speech. Unlike the child who is unaware of his disfluencies, this child may be trying to *ignore* the repetitions or prolongations in his efforts to communicate. In this situation, his parents are not over-reacting to his speech, because his disfluencies are atypical and do call attention to themselves.

It is important to note that a child may appear normally disfluent during the evaluation, but his parents report he is abnormally disfluent at home. In this case the clinician should inform the family that he hears primarily normal disfluencies although he realizes the child's speech may be different at home. As a result, the clinician should treat the child as if he is abnormally disfluent. When a child's speech appears abnormal to the clinician, this impression needs to be communicated to the parents and then treatment should be prescribed. Telling parents their child's speech is normal when it is obviously not may make them resist suggestions for therapy.

THE EVALUATION PROCEDURE

The clinician is usually contacted by concerned parents who have witnessed an increase in their child's disfluencies during the preceding weeks or months. The parents frequently state that someone has told them to ignore the disfluencies, and they have done so, but without noticing a decrease in the speech problem. They are now seeking additional help.

The clinician may want to analyze a child's speech early in the interview and under different conditions. First, the child can play with toys, read books, or talk to puppets. Another therapist may enter the room and start to play, but accelerate the activities and interrupt the child while he is conversing. Then, the parents can join the play situation while the second clinician departs. After awhile, an outsider can request that the parents leave the room to "check something." By creating what can be stressful situations, one can assess the effect pressure has on a child's disfluency. The clinician will also want to study the parents' reactions to their child's speech. Overt gestures and signs of uneasiness, impatience, and concern, and the child's reaction to these behaviors, should be noted. When the parents are again alone with the clinician, they should be asked to describe the disfluency they heard and to judge whether it is typical of or different from the speech pattern they hear at home.

If the child is normally disfluent with the clinician and his parents concur that this is the way he speaks at home, counseling emphasis should be directed toward alleviating the parents' concern, assuring them that their child is normally disfluent, and eliminating possible inappropriate reactions to their child's normal speech patterns. Only two sections of the management program, which concentrate specifically on the parents' response to their child's speech, need to be reviewed. (Refer to "Selecting Program Sections" in Chapter III.) It is most likely that the clinician will treat normally disfluent children far *less* often than he will treat abnormally disfluent youngsters, because parents usually react to abnormal disfluencies more often than they overrespond to normal speech patterns. Whether or not possible overreactions from parents can move a child from normal to abnormal disfluencies continues to be a point of contention, but the possibility exists in at least a few cases (Van Riper, 1971). Therefore, the clinician needs to monitor carefully the overconcerned or overcritical parents to guard against their creation of a problem.

If the clinician observes that the child is abnormally disfluent, and his parents report that his speech is similar at home, the parents may benefit from the complete counseling program in this text. Initially parents may need the opportunity to vent their feelings concerning their child's speech. In many cases, parents have a sense of guilt that suggests they are responsible for their child's speech difficulty. The clinician should remember that there is no conclusive evidence to support this cause/effect relationship, and there is no better way to increase the parents' anxieties than to corroborate their expressions of responsibility. The clinician's purpose is not to instill or support feelings of depression, anxiety, hostility, or guilt, but to counsel parents that the causal factors of what they have termed "stuttering" are not known. The clinician can explain that all children are disfluent to different degrees. The reason(s) for this variation may be the result of a combination of factors or environmental conditions, but disfluency can occur even when these factors and conditions do not seem to exist. The clinician might add, however, that there is considerable authoritative support that creating a home environment that is conducive to fluency and language maturation with minimal environmental and speech pressures frequently helps a child spontaneously recover from his speech difficulty.

In summary, the following four points need to be stressed to parents:

1. We do not know the reasons why their child is having difficulty speaking, although experience tells us certain factors may be more important than others.
2. It is of little value to concentrate on "How could this have happened?" or "What did we do wrong?" unless these questions are used positively to help identify possible areas for improvement.
3. Based upon current practice, an important aspect of the therapy plan includes maintaining a home free from environmental and speech pressures.
4. The clinician will attempt to direct the parents' efforts in creating this type of environment.

After the parents have had an opportunity to express their concerns and hopefully their willingness to participate in the program, the clinician may begin to obtain information about their home. It will aid the clinician to determine if both parents are receptive to suggestions for child management and if they might benefit from the information provided in this program, and to attempt to identify obvious, as well as not so obvious, environmental pressures or communicative stress.

Certain pressures may be apparent and may seem directly related to the child's disfluencies: for example, when the child is disfluent his mother spanks him, yells at him to "stop and start over," or fills in a word for him. Some pressures may be semi-apparent and may be indirectly related to the child's speech. For instance, when the child talks, his older brother frequently interjects, and no one intercedes. Other pressures may be nonapparent and difficult to identify. For example, the child is subconsciously worried that he cannot meet the demands for effective communication, or the child is confused by the inconsistency with which reinforcement and punishment are administered by his parents.

The parent interview not only should aid in determining how parents react to their child's speech when he is disfluent, but also should be utilized to explore their daily routine. Because it is the primary purpose of this program to help parents manage their child in everyday situations, information regarding their daily activities, from awakening to bedtime, is essential. By reviewing this routine, specific problems may be identified. Although general questions such as "Can you describe your home situation?" or "Do you have problems managing your child?" may elicit some information, they may not identify the small, but everyday, problems of child-rearing. The clinician must determine, for example, if bedtime is a difficult period for the child and his parents; if morning is hectic when the child must be ready for school; and if there are problems at the dinner table when everyone wants to talk at the same time and no one wants to eat his spinach.

PRE/POST PROGRAM RATING SCALE

The Pre/Post Program Rating Scale (see Appendix I) should be completed by the parents during the evaluation so that the clinician can better assess their reactions to their child's disfluencies and the way they manage their child. It is important that the parents complete the Rating Scale by putting a mark next to the word most descriptive of the frequency with which each behavior occurs. Make note of those areas that may need to be explored in more detail. The Rating Scale should again be completed following the program to determine if there has been a change in the parents' attitude and/or responses to their child's speech and behavior.

CHAPTER 3

Treatment of Abnormal and Normal Disfluency: A Child Management Program

Whether early stuttering has been hypothesized to result from a neurosis (Barbara, 1954), diagnosogenic paradigm (Johnson, 1959), word and situation fears (Wishner, 1950), an anticipatory struggle reaction (Bloodstein, 1975a), or an approach-avoidance conflict (Sheehan, 1975), or is shaped by operant conditioning (Shames and Sherrick, 1963), the primary focus of all the hypotheses is centered on the parents' possible negative effect on their child and the child's response to his parents' actions. Therefore, from different theoretical positions has evolved the common recommendation to reduce environmental pressures, especially those that exist between parent and child. Even if there is the possibility of coordination difficulty (Zaleski, 1965) or a motoric speech system that has not fully stabilized, therapeutic emphasis is still directed toward changing the home environment so that it is more conducive to fluent speech and to the development of fluency. This includes reducing communicative stress, which may result from pressures on the child's speech as well as from the reward and punishment regimen established for "good" and "bad" behaviors. The necessity for a fair and equitable discipline system in a disfluent child's home has been emphasized repeatedly (Johnson, 1949; Van Riper, 1963; Luper and Mulder, 1965; Emerick and Hatten, 1974; Bloodstein, 1975b). However, general suggestions or case studies, rather than detailed methods, are usually presented. Interestingly, it is the behavioral psychology literature that has provided a more thorough review of discipline methods that seem feasible for incorporation into a counseling program for parents with a disfluent child.

15

In order to help parents implement an effective management system and strengthen a child's self-concept, behavioral psychology seems to emphasize the identification of appropriate behaviors, the employment of praise and reinforcement to increase these responses, and the elimination of physical punishment. One method of achieving these goals consists of counseling parents; the other involves them directly in a reinforcement paradigm. O'Dell (1974) reviewed the literature and found that counseling approaches have most commonly been in the form of advice and verbal direction (Patterson, 1965; Wahler et al., 1965; Hawkins et al., 1966; Allen and Harris 1971). Programmed instruction texts have also been used widely to present the principles of effective child management (Lindsley, 1966; Patterson and Gullion, 1968; Smith and Smith, 1968; Cohen, 1970; Becker, 1971; Hall, 1974). In contrast to a didactic approach, some studies have directly trained mothers to modify their reactions to their child's behavior by tallying the times they reinforced or ignored target behaviors. Wahler et al. (1965) instructed mothers to move from responding to their child's inappropriate behaviors to reinforcing opposite, incompatible, positive responses, at least within the confines of an experimental setting. Baseline and follow-up data revealed that the inappropriate behavior was extinguished for lack of reinforcement while the target response increased in frequency. Herbert and Baer (1972) trained mothers at home to count episodes of attention to appropriate behaviors and found that this method increased their frequency of response to these behaviors.

Point or token reinforcement systems are a more tangible form of reinforcement and have also been employed to increase desirable behaviors. Christophersen et al. (1972) utilized a point reinforcement system consisting of a list, formulated by parents, of appropriate and inappropriate behaviors. The child either earned or lost points for engaging in particular activities. Parents made a list of privileges they thought their child would want and set the amount of points required to obtain each reward.

Several authorities feel that punishment may be necessary for some behaviors. Zeilburger et al. (1968) and Patterson and Gullion (1968) suggested that an undesirable behavior may be weakened by ignoring it, or that a child could usually be punished effectively by sending him to his room for a "time out" period. Becker (1971) added that only when the child engaged in activities that were physically harmful to himself or others was spanking possibly justified.

In summary, behavioral psychology has provided us with specific suggestions to implement what authorities in the area of stuttering have recommended, namely, to define rules so that the child knows what is expected of him, to utilize reinforcement and praise to maintain desirable behaviors, and to establish a non-injurious discipline system for a child's misbehaviors by either ignoring inappropriate responses or non-physically punishing him.

Blaunstein and Wahler (1971) have utilized three of these principles when counseling parents of disfluent children— defining rules, a "time out" period, and a reward point system. They found that parents reported a decrease in their child's disfluencies and an improved interrelationship with each other.

DEVELOPMENT AND TESTING
OF THE CHILD MANAGEMENT PROGRAM

Over a three-year period, a child management program for parents concerned with their child's disfluency was developed and tested. In its final form it contained those principles that could be included in one program. Although most of the program was didactic in form, parent performance could be monitored with the questionnaires, rating scale, and checklists included in the program.

In a preliminary study summarized briefly here, the program was administered to the parents of fifteen abnormally disfluent children to determine whether or not it eliminated or significantly reduced their children's disfluencies and whether or not their general home environment improved. The children ranged in age between three years two months and four years nine months. The program was completed in eight to twelve weeks. Each child was seen before program administration and a percentage of abnormally disfluent words over words spoken was obtained during a 30-minute play session with his parents and the clinician. Abnormal disfluencies were defined as either prolongations longer than one second or two or more repetitions of one syllable or less. A percentage was again obtained after the program was completed, and pre- and post-program percentages were compared. In six children there was essentially a cessation of abnormal disfluencies, that is, a level estimated to be 3 percent or less. With six children there was a notable reduction in the number of abnormal disfluencies, and in three children the frequency of disfluencies remained essentially the same.

A rating scale was completed by each of the parents before and after program administration in order to determine if there were changes in the way they managed their child or responded to his speech. By their responses on the rating scale, all parents indicated that they had understood and were generally implementing the suggestions outlined in the program. Seven parents reported a return to normal speech, and five a decrease in their child's disfluencies as well as a decrease in the tension or effort associated with speaking. One parent observed significant improvement in her child's speech but felt disfluency continued to interfere with his communication. Two parents reported little or no change at home. The discrepancy between clinic tabulations and parent reports may have resulted from the subjectivity of parent opinion or the error factor inherent in the clinical analysis of disfluencies.

Each child was re-evaluated six months after the termination of therapy. One of the six children who had been fluent at the end of the program was again abnormally disfluent; however, another child who had been as disfluent following the program as before was now fluent. The children who had different degrees of speech improvement after program administration continued to be more fluent than before the procedure was introduced.

This type of analysis must be interpreted cautiously, because the lack of controls inherent in home program administration, the variability of disfluency over time, the subjectivity of rating scales, and the uncertainty still surrounding the relationship between home environment and disfluency must be considered. However, the program's value for establishing a more consistent, more pleasurable and peaceful home environment with a minimal degree of communicative stress is worthy of attention. In twelve cases the child's disfluencies were reduced considerably or returned to within prescribed limits, possibly as the result of an improved home environment. In the other cases either the parents may have failed to expedite the program, as they reported, or the children may have failed to profit from it.

This program was field-tested in order to determine whether or not other clinicians could effectively administer it without prior formal instruction. Based upon the experience of three clinicians, each providing the procedure to two families, the program could be competently and efficaciously administered, and reduction of abnormal disfluencies to within prescribed limits in two children and a decrease with another three youngsters appeared to be related to the therapeutic process.

PURPOSE OF THE PROGRAM

The primary program objective is to develop consistency in the everyday routine of parent and child in order to create as conducive an atmosphere for fluent speech as possible. Parents are instructed in ways to manage their child so that he knows the regulations governing his home environment and also recognizes that the rules do not change from moment to moment or day to day. For example, when he starts to talk he is assured that he will not be interrupted by others; likewise, the same will be expected of him when others are speaking. If he misbehaves, his parents will use specific, predictable, and non-injurious measures to deal with his misbehavior. If he does his chores he will be consistently rewarded according to a predetermined system. Essentially, his environment should be loving, tolerant of minor infractions, have sufficient praise for jobs well done, and be a shelter to which he can bring his problems and seek comfort.

The identification and treatment of covert factors in a child's environment are not discussed in this text; rather, concrete and overt suggestions on child management are offered, and the recommendations outlined in the program are organized as a core procedure for managing the disfluent child. This program emphasizes the treatment of the child's general environment in addition to identifying specific factors that appear to effect fluency. There are two reasons for this approach. First, a child may be more disfluent every time he is excited, nervous, angry, or someone interrupts him, but he may also be disfluent even though he seems to be having a "good time" or is under no apparent pressure. Momentary periods of happiness may not be sufficient to reduce disfluencies if a child's day is filled with inconsistency. Only when a child repeatedly experiences consistency and understanding in his interaction with his parents can he feel truly secure in any one situation because he knows what to expect in the future. Second, what is important to the child is not necessarily of concern to the adult. A youngster may cry for reasons that seem minor to parents, yet in reality may be very important to the child. For example, a child could react with the same intensity to losing a toy truck that the adult would display if his house were destroyed by fire. A child may take a "play" situation as seriously as the adult takes a business negotiation with an important client. It would be difficult to try to determine all the factors that may evoke a child's negative reaction. However, certain characteristics in the environment can be identified that would be offensive to *both* the parent and child, and these factors should be eliminated. If a parent would not like others to do something to him, why should he do it to his child? For example, no adult would like to be ridiculed for speaking poorly, to be continually told "no," to be yelled at for something that is insignificant, to be seldom praised, or to be treated unfairly by the law.

ADMINISTERING THE PROGRAM

This program is a guide for the experienced clinician to help parents manage their child; it is not a detailed or cookbook approach to family counseling. Questions will arise that will need to be answered, and each professional must decide if he or she has had sufficient experience in counseling parents to administer this program effectively.

If there are two parents, both should attend each session if at all possible. It is frequently difficult for one parent to tell the other parent how to change a behavior. The mere fact that one partner is telling the other to change may build a certain amount of resentment or resistance to the suggestions. In addition, it is risky to assume one parent will convey the suggestions completely or accurately. In cases where there is one parent and another person who is close to the child, sessions should include both people if possible.

The following program sections are essentially self-explanatory. In every section, the author has provided a detailed discussion for implementation of each step in the prodecure and has also included answers to the more common questions that parents asked when the program was tested. The clinician should thoroughly review each of the sections before presenting them to the parents. Each section has been simplified, and certain paragraphs may seem repetitious, but they are included to emphasize a point.

PROGRAM SECTIONS

The program is divided into seven sections of child management, and these sections can be separated into two parts. Whether the clinician administers only Sections I and II of Part I, or both Parts I and II will likely be predicated on the features of a child's disfluency and the specific characteristics of the home environment. Selecting the appropriate program sections is discussed under the next heading.

PART I

SECTIONS I AND II—How parents can react to their child when he is disfluent, and how they can deal with speaking demands in the environment.

SECTION III—How parents can increase their child's self-concept and feeling of security.

PART II

SECTION IV—How parents can react to their child when he unintentionally misbehaves.

SECTION V—How parents can react to their child when he intentionally misbehaves.

SECTION VI—How parents can establish consistency when responding to their child's misbehaviors.

SECTION VII—How parents can reinforce (reward) their child when he does what they request (i.e., does chores, plays well with siblings). This includes use of a star chart.

SELECTING APPROPRIATE PROGRAM SECTIONS

For the Normally Disfluent Child

Parents of the child who is clearly normally disfluent may only need to follow the principles in Sections I and II. After receiving these suggestions, they should return in one month for a re-evaluation. In the meantime, they can contact the clinician if their child's disfluency increases significantly, but they should be aware that usually there is some fluctuation in severity. They may hear more disfluency some days than others, but this is normal and may not be related to any particular situation. If their child's speech changes for several consecutive days, then they should contact the clinician.

For the Abnormally Disfluent Child

The number of sections that should be provided to parents will depend upon the information obtained during the initial evaluation. The management program is divided purposely into two parts: Sections I to III are concerned with the child's speech, self-concept, and security. Sections IV to VII deal with the child's misbehavior, consistent discipline, and the establishment of a reinforcement system for target behaviors. The following guidelines should be followed when deciding whether Part I alone or both Parts I and II should be provided.

1. Part I of the program can be administered to most parents with or without Part II. Even if communicative stress appears low, discipline is not a problem, and the everyday home routine appears to be a smooth one, three or four sessions will need to be scheduled as a precautionary measure to review, if not to present, the principles in Sections I, II, and III. Often there will be several suggestions that will be new or a vague concept will be crystalized.

2. Both parts of the program can be administered if the parents are having difficulties with discipline (i.e., their child fails to "listen" to them) or problems with his refusal to perform daily activities (i.e., brush teeth, get ready for school, go to bed, play well with sibling), or the parents administer discipline inconsistently, so that at one time they yell, another time spank, another time ignore, and another time accept a misbehavior or the child's failure to do what is requested. Guidelines are needed so that the child knows what is expected of him and what will happen if he does or does not do what is asked. Part II is not intended to make little robots out of children, but to establish an environment where they know what to anticipate and are consistently reinforced when they meet these expectations. The clinician can guide parents in establishing fair and equitable expectations for their child, then he can show them how to obtain adherence to those guidelines in an atmosphere of fairness, love, and reinforcement.

3. There are several situations where Part II is not provided, even though the child is abnormally disfluent.

   A. Of course, if the parents appear to be maintaining a consistent and fair home environment where discipline and daily routines are not a problem, Part II need not be provided.

   B. The home situation appears to warrant other professional services. The clinician may feel there are unusual environmental factors or that the parents, the child, or both display personality difficulties that would impede the acquisition of program principles. However, if possible, Part I of the program can be provided before, or along with such a referral.

   C. Part I can be employed as a "trial period of therapy" during which a decision can be reached on the efficacy of providing Part II. In a few cases, the clinician may suspect parental resistance to program principles or environmental factors, such as a questionable child/parent relationship, which may be preventing a family from benefiting from the program. In this case, patient reassessment of therapeutic goals is necessary after Section III is provided, and referral, a new direction in therapy, or termination of counseling may be considered.

   D. Infrequently, the clinician may find parents who have difficulty understanding the principles in this program—a certain degree of sophistication is required to follow the program accurately. In these situations, Part I should be provided, but if the parents appear unusually confused, Part II may need to be summarized and only a few pertinent suggestions reviewed.

SCHEDULE FOR PROGRAM ADMINISTRATION

If the entire program is to be administered, it is likely Sections I, II, III, IV, and VI can be presented at weekly intervals, but an additional week or weeks may be required if the parents have difficulty modifying their environment or find they must make major alterations in their home to accommodate the suggestions.

Section V (How to React When your Child Intentionally Misbehaves) will require at least a two-week period to implement, since punishment is a complex area and will require considerable explanation. Section VII (Star Chart) will also take two to three weeks, since the clinician will want to follow the parents over time as they institute the chart.

Experience revealed that the therapeutic session was best divided into two parts. The first half of the session was used to review the previous section and problems concerning its implementation. The clinician frequently needed to clarify and/or expand on some points and may have had to explore specific issues that arose when the new guidelines were introduced at home. The second half of the session was reserved for discussion of the new section to be incorporated into the home during the following week.

Each section of the program should be presented and summarized for the parents. The clinician may wish to outline in writing the major points of discussion for their reference at home. As needed, after each principle, the clinician can ask if there are any questions.

The parents should be presented with only one section at a time since they need to concentrate on each section, and too much information at once may overwhelm them.

Each day parents should set aside time to discuss the new principles and whether or not they have followed them. They can review any problems that occurred during the day, and, if there are questions, they should feel free to contact the clinician for clarification.

As sections are added, *all* principles (the present ones and those from previous weeks) should be reviewed daily. The clinician should emphasize to the parents that they need to continue following preceding sections as well as to incorporate the most recent information.

QUESTIONNAIRES AND CHECKLISTS

A separate questionnaire is provided with each section of the program. The parents should take the questionnaire home, fill it out together, preferably on the same day as the counseling session, review it during the week, and bring it to the next meeting. If necessary, they may look at their notes to find the answers. Answers to the questionnaire appear in Appendix II.

In addition, a checklist for each section is provided for the parents to chart daily how frequently they engage in a particular behavior. If a behavior did not occur during the day, they are to place a "0" in the appropriate square. If a behavior is irrelevant, that is, the statement does not apply because a situation that would evoke this action did not occur, then have them mark an "X". For example, if their child was well-behaved all day, statements such as "Remained calm when your child misbehaved" or "Sent your child to his room for five minutes" have no relevance. Have both parents fill out the checklist, but each parent should use a different color of ink, so that the clinician can better monitor each parent. Preferably both parents can complete this checklist at the end of each day. Its primary function is to guide them in monitoring their own behavior and to help the clinician estimate how well they are incorporating the principles of child management. In order not to burden the parents, they should not be required to fill out the checklist throughout the day, but rather to select the most convenient time in the evening.

CHAPTER 4

Child Management
Program

SECTION I

How to Deal With Your Child's Speech

A. Disfluency—How to React

If your child is disfluent *do not*:

1. Hit your child
2. Tell your child to "stop stuttering"
3. Threaten punishment for "poor" speech
4. Help your child with the word
5. Tell your child to speak more slowly
6. Tell your child to think about what he is going to say
7. Answer or "fill in" for your child
8. Look concerned
9. Appear angry or impatient

Engaging in these actions does not help your child; instead it gives him the impression that you are dissatisfied with him and the way he communicates. You may also make him feel that disfluencies are "bad" and should be avoided. Of course, this is not so. In addition, you will be calling attention to his speech pattern.

Do:

Try to act as though your child is speaking fluently. Remain calm and pay attention to *what* your child is saying. Try to show him that you enjoy talking with him and at least seem interested in what he has to say, even though you may not be.

If your child is extremely excited and seems to be in a hurry to tell you something, you may say "take it easy" or "take your time," "keep calm," "don't get so excited"; then follow with "I have time and I want to hear what you have to say." *Note*: This is different than telling your child to speak more slowly. In this way you do not refer to your child's speech but rather to the fact that he is too excited. You want him generally to slow down, *not* just to speak more slowly. You do not mention his speech but refer only to the fact he is too excited and needs to take his time.

B. Listen to Your Child When He Is Talking to You

When your child comes to you while you are busy cooking, cleaning, reading, etc., stop what you are doing and give him your full attention so that he does not have to compete with your activity. However, you do not have to do this immediately each time your child speaks. Usually your child can wait a minute until you finish your activity, but you should:

1. Tell him you will soon listen to him after you finish what you are doing. You can say, "I want to know what you're telling me, and I will listen to what you have to say in a minute, but I must finish this right now."
2. Try to find a convenient stopping place in your activity so you do not keep your child waiting for an unnecessarily long period (over one to two minutes).
3. Give your child your full attention when you do listen to him. Look at him; respond to what he is saying.

Crying, temper tantrums, and nagging should be ignored* after you have explained to him you will listen when you are finished with your present activity. You may again repeat that you must finish what you are doing before you listen to him, but do not continually tell him this or engage in arguments. Although he may not have the concept of "minute" or "second," he will soon learn that he only has to wait a short time before you give him your attention. He will then probably be more willing to wait for you to finish your activity.

Extreme caution should be exercised not to pay more attention to your child when he comes to you and is disfluent than when he comes to you and is fluent. You should have him wait the same length of time in both situations and be equally willing to listen to what he has to say.

If possible, sit down with your child when you talk with him so you will be face to face. This will allow him to feel you are at his level instead of an adult figure above and away from him.

If your child demands a longer period of attention after you have been with him a couple of minutes, tell him that you

---

* Ignore means not to pay attention to any negative behavior no matter what he does unless he destroys objects or hurts himself or others.

must get back to what you are doing. Tell him that you will see him later after you are through with your activity. Go back to your task; do not argue, and ignore any crying or yelling.

These rules should apply to any other children in the family.

Section I—Questionnaire

Please fill out this questionnaire and bring it to the next session.

Name _____ Date_____

1. When my child is talking to me while I am cooking I should
   1) _____
   _____.
   2) _____
   _____.

2. When my child is *disfluent*, I should give him the (same, more, or less) attention than when he is *fluent*.

3. When my child is disfluent I will not
   1)_____.
   2)_____.
   3)_____.
   4)_____.
   5)_____.
   6)_____.

4. Should I immediately stop what I am doing each time my child speaks to me?
   Yes_____ No_____

5. If I do not stop my activity immediately when my child starts talking, what should I do?

   _____
   _____
   _____.

6. What would I say if my child came to me and was extremely excited? (More than one choice is correct.)
   a) "take it easy"
   b) "speak slowly"
   c) "don't get so excited"
   d) "don't speak so fast"

7. When my child is disfluent, I:
   1)_____.
   2)_____.
   3)_____.

Section I—Checklist

Child's Name: _____ Date: _____

Write number of times each behavior occured, a 0 if it did not occur, and an X if statement is irrelevant.

	Mon.	Tues.	Wed.	Thur.	Fri.	Sat.	Sun.	Mon.	Tues.	Wed.	Thur.	Fri.	Sat.	Sun.
Spanked my child when he was disfluent														
Told my child to "stop stuttering"														
Helped my child with a disfluent word														
Told my child to speak more slowly														
Paid attention to what my child was saying each time he spoke														
Stopped immediately what I was doing each time my child spoke to me														
Told my child to wait until I was through doing _____, and then I would listen to him														
Ignored crying if my child wanted my attention immediately														
Ignored temper tantrums														
Had my child wait for my attention the same length of time whether he was fluent or disfluent														

SECTION II

How to Deal With Your
Child's Speech (continued)

A. Taking Turns to Talk

Our lives and homes are increasingly demanding; consequently, our speech patterns are often hurried, with intermittent interruptions. Frequently the small child learning language is unable to meet both the competency and time demands. To avoid these communicative pressures, all members of the family should take turns to talk. When one person is talking, others should wait. A child who is continually interrupted by others when he is talking, or *feels* he *may* be interrupted while he is speaking, is under pressure to communicate. In order to reduce this pressure, your child needs to know that when he has the floor no one will interfere. A child who interrupts while others are speaking should be told, "When _____ is finished, it will be your turn, and no one will interrupt you." Apply this rule to everyone in the family.

If a child is disfluent while trying to interrupt you, *continue* talking. Disfluency is not an excuse for a child to interject into your conversation—and be careful not to give him the floor faster when he is disfluent than when he is fluent.

Parents should role play both taking turns and interrupting each other. The parent who interrupts should be told he must wait until the other person is finished talking. Brothers and sisters should be guided to allow each other to have the floor and to wait for their turns.

If your child continues talking for an unusually long period, stop him and tell him it is someone else's turn and he will have time to talk again when other people have spoken. If he continues talking or demanding the floor, ignore him and let someone else speak.

B. Avoid Using the Term "Stuttering"

Do not use the term "stuttering" to describe your child's speech when talking with him or others. "Stuttering" denotes an abnormal speech pattern that is often severely disfluent

35

and characterized by long hesitations, blocks, and facial grimaces. The individual is conscious of his speech and usually is very concerned about it, which in turn may affect his verbal interaction with others. Since this description does not apply to your child, do not use the term "stuttering."

Tell other children in the family, relatives, and friends not to use the word "stuttering" and explain to them how to react to disfluent speech as you have learned in Sections I and II.

C. Avoid Talking About the Past

Avoid questioning your child about past situations unless he initiates the conversation. Young children are usually more interested in the present and future than in the past. Besides, talking about the past is more abstract and therefore more difficult to do. For example, when your child comes home from school, avoid specific questions about what he *did* at school unless he brings up something he would like to discuss. Also avoid questions about what he did at the circus, grandma's, or the playground unless he voluntarily offers information. In order to show interest a general question such as "How was school?" or "How was the circus?" is appropriate when you greet your child, but accept a brief answer such as "fine" or "okay," and do not question him further if he seems at all uninterested in discussing his day.

D. Avoid Command Performances

Avoid placing demands on your child to recite. If he wants to say his favorite nursery rhyme, count to ten, or say the ABC's, then fine. However, do not expect him to perform or recite, especially in front of a group of people or for strangers.

Section II—Questionnaire

Please fill out this questionnaire and bring it to the next session.

Name _____ Date_____

1. I do not use the term "stuttering" in front of my child, but I can use it when talking to others.
   True_____ False_____

2. Talking about future events _____ or past events _____ is likely to be easier for my child.

3. When members of the family are conversing, each person should _____ _____ to talk.

4. When grandma comes over, insist that your child say his ABC's or his favorite nursery rhyme if he knows them very well.
   True_____ False_____

5. If your child is disfluent while he is trying to interrupt, you should:

   a) give him your attention immediately
   b) tell him to stop stuttering
   c) continue talking
   d) tell him to speak more slowly

6. Which is the more abstract type of conversation, talking about the present _____ or the past _____?

7. Describe the term "stuttering."

   _____

   _____.

8. Does the answer you gave to question 7 describe the way your child speaks?
   Yes_____ No_____

9. To show interest in your child's activities, you can ask your child:

   a) "What did you do today?"
   b) "How's school?"
   c) "Tell me everything you did today."

10. What should you do if your child talks for a long time and someone else wants the floor?

    _____.

11. If your child wants to say a nursery rhyme, stop him for fear he may be disfluent.
    True_____ False_____

Section II—Checklist

Child's Name _____ Date: _____

Write number of times each behavior occurred, a 0 if it did not occur, and an X if statement is irrelevant.

	Mon.	Tues.	Wed.	Thurs.	Fri.	Sat.	Sun.	Mon.	Tues.	Wed.	Thur.	Fri.	Sat.	Sun.
Referred to my child's disfluencies as "stuttering"														
Insisted that he recite a nursery rhyme														
Helped my child with a difficult word														
Told my child that he would have to wait until I was through doing ____														
Ignored temper tantrums														
Spanked my child when he was disfluent														
When he interrupted, I told my child that he would have to wait until it was his turn to talk														
Told others not to interrupt while someone else was talking														
Parents pretended both to interrupt and to take turns talking														

SECTION III

How to Improve Self-Concept and Security

A. Building Self-Respect

Praise is an excellent means of building self-confidence. It counteracts criticism of a child's misbehaviors which can damage his self-concept. Find activities your child does well and tell him he has done a good job. Praise him for helping you and for performing his chores, especially if he does them without being told to do so, or praise him for drawing a nice picture. Find at least two things a day that warrant praise; however, make sure your remarks are honest, sincere, and appropriate.

If your child frequently engages in an activity you do not like, praise him when he is doing the opposite, positive act as well as punishing him for the negative act. For example, you may punish or reprimand your children when they are fighting but also praise them when they play nicely.

B. Reduce the Word "No" (or Any Negative Response, Such as "Don't," "Can't," or "Stop It")

"No" can be one of the most common words you use when talking to your child. Used too often this word loses significance and becomes frustrating, punishing, and hurting. Think about how serious a misbehavior actually is before you condemn it with "no." Can you actually tolerate what he is doing because his actions will not result in harm to himself or others, will not result in damage to your property, and will last a short period of time? Or can you switch your child's attention to another activity he might also find interesting?

C. Time Period Alone—A Time to Release the Child's Pent-up Feelings

Times alone with your child will build security, closeness, and help bring out things that are bothering him. Once every day, one parent and the child should have a five- to ten-minute session alone (without brothers and sisters). A reading time, a walk, or playing with toys are good activities to share together. The sessions should be relaxed and leisurely; for this reason they probably are best scheduled in the evening before bedtime.

During the session, casually ask your child *how* the day went. Please note that you should ask *how* the day went and not *what* he did today. You want your child to tell you about his feelings, not about his activities.

You may also wish to ask specific questions if your child is reluctant to respond to the general question "How did the day go?" For example, you can ask:

"Did you have a good day?"
"Did you and Mommy have a good day?"
"Did you and (your brother or sister) have a nice time today?"
"Did you like nursery school today?"

Be sure not to *force* your child to tell you about his day. After asking him two or three questions and obtaining little response, stop the questions. You only want to set an atmosphere that is conducive to his telling you his problems, if he has any, but you should not demand that he do so. Perhaps tomorrow he will feel more like conversing.

When your child tells you about a situation that is bothering him, do not berate him for what he did or how he reacted. He may feel you are judging him for confiding in you. You want him to feel free to release any feelings he is keeping inside. You should not try to convince your child that he is wrong in feeling the way he does, tell him "big boys and girls" do not feel that way, or he should not feel that way about Mommy. Instead, either present a simple solution if one is available; or, if the problem is complex, calmly recognize that the situation bothers him by saying, "I guess *(situation)* really upsets you"; "I can see that bothers you"; or "I guess *(name of brother, sister, father, mother, friend, etc.)* can really make you angry."

Note that you are not agreeing or disagreeing, you are simply allowing him to further express his feelings. Repeat these phrases as he tells you about the situation. If you do agree with what he is saying, you may add, "That would make me angry" or "I don't blame you for getting upset."

You may wish to chat with your child more frequently than once a day, especially if he is having a particularly bad day. Take him aside, sit down, and have a brief conversation together that employs the procedure described above.

Section III—Questionnaire

Please fill out this questionnaire and bring it to the next session.

Name _____ Date_____

1. What is a better question to ask your child during the time period alone?

   a) "What did you do today?"
   b) "How did the day go?"

2. If possible, try to tolerate some misbehaviors, especially if your child will not hurt himself or others, will not damage property, and his behavior does not last for a long time.
   True_____ False_____

3. How long should you spend alone with your child each day? _____ minutes or more.

4. If your child does not wish to respond to "Did you and Mommy have a good day?"

   a) Keep on drilling him until he tells you what's on his mind.
   b) Stop questioning. You only wanted to give him a chance to talk about any problems.

5. If your child frequently does not scrub his teeth without being told to do so, you should _____ _____ when he does scrub his teeth on his own.

6. What may happen if you use the word "no" too often?
   1) _____
   _____.
   2) _____
   _____.

7. Praise your child even if he did something carelessly.
   True_____ False_____

8. During the time period alone, what type of question can you ask your child?
   Example: _____
   _____.

9. Praise your child at least _____ times a day.

42

Section III—Checklist

Child's Name _____ Date: _____

Write number of times each behavior occurred, a 0 if it did not occur, and an X if statement is irrelevant.

	Mon.	Tues.	Wed.	Thur.	Fri.	Sat.	Sun.	Mon.	Tues.	Wed.	Thur.	Fri.	Sat.	Sun.
Praised my child for something that he did well														
Used negative responses ("no," "can't," "stop it")														
Spent at least 5–10 minutes alone with my child														
Pressured my child to converse by asking many questions														
Asked the question "How did the day go?"														
Asked the question "What did you do today?"														
Took turns talking														
Told my child to "stop stuttering"														
Told my child to speak more slowly														

43

SECTION IV

How to React When Your Child Unintentionally Misbehaves

Your child will probably get into mischief *without meaning to do so*. For example, he will spill his milk, get mud on his new coat, splash water on the bathroom floor, or squirt glue on the rug. Although it may seem apparent to you that your child should know better, he still winds up in trouble.

When your child does something that annoys you, you should take the following actions:

1. Ask yourself how serious the misbehavior is. Be tolerant of those behaviors that may be irritating but that do not result in harm to your child or others, do not result in permanent damage to property, occur infrequently, and are not done maliciously or intentionally.
2. Deal with a misbehavior with calmness and collectiveness.
3. Can you switch your child's attention to an acceptable activity?
4. Be sure you do not attack your child personally; instead, refer to the wrongful act he has committed.
5. *Do not harp on what already has been done—that will not change the situation.*
6. Do not ask him *why* he did this or "How could you have done this?" because he probably does not know. Such questions pin your child in a corner and do not derive answers.
7. Present a rectifying solution to the misbehavior if at all possible. Give your child the opportunity to make amends for an accident by helping you clean up.
8. Tell your child that what he has done makes you angry. Feel free to express your feelings openly. However, after you have expressed your feelings, present a rectifying solution.

    Example:
    Situation: Child spills milk

Wrong Action: Mother says, "Why did you do this? You know better. You are clumsy. You are a bad boy (girl)."
Situation: Child spills milk
Right Action: Mother says, "You spilled your milk. Mom gets angry (or does not like it) when this happens, but here is a cloth, you can help Mommy clean it up."

Note: By expressing your feelings this way, you are: 1) describing the wrong act, 2) stating that it makes you angry, and 3) presenting a solution to the wrong act.

In order for a misbehavior to be classified as unintentional, it should occur infrequently. After offering a solution to a misbehavior three or four times, you may determine that your child either is actually misbehaving intentionally or is unduly careless—although you should make this decision carefully.

If a misbehavior occurs *repeatedly and carelessly,* then you should punish your child. Also, if he refuses to help correct the situation, you should punish him. This means sending him to his room (which is discussed in Section V). If necessary, use the form of punishment you have been using until now, but at the next session you will learn a better way to punish your child—sending him to his room for a "time out" period.

Children often make too much noise, at least as far as their parents are concerned. Being noisy might be considered a form of unintentional misbehavior, but not really, since children frequently play and yell in the car and at home. However, at times shouting and loud games can be irritating, and *rewarding* periods when your child plays quietly may prove to be more effective than punishing the times he is noisy. Ways to reward quiet play are discussed in Section VII.

Section IV—Questionnaire

Please complete this questionnaire and bring it to the next session.

Name _____ Date_____

1. When your child does something that annoys you, *which* actions should you take? (Check the ones you would do)

    a) Present a way your child can correct a misbehavior.
    b) Tell your child that his action makes you angry.
    c) Spank your child, since he should know better.
    d) Be accepting of some misbehaviors if they are not serious.
    e) Ask your child *why* he was so careless.
    f) Refer only to the wrongful act when you reprimand your child.
    g) Tell your child he was a "bad boy (girl)."
    h) Keep calm and do not lose your temper.

2. If your child continually gets glue in the rug, this could be considered:

    a) an intentional misbehavior
    b) an unintentional misbehavior
    c) both

Section IV—Checklist

Name: _____   Date: _____

Write number of times each behavior occurred, a 0 if it did not occur, and an X if statement is irrelevant.

	Mon.	Tues.	Wed.	Thur.	Fri.	Sat.	Sun.	Mon.	Tues.	Wed.	Thur.	Fri.	Sat.	Sun.
When my child misbehaved, I asked him why he did it														
Told my child he was a "bad boy"														
Remained calm when my child misbehaved														
Presented a way my child could correct a misbehavior														
Referred only to the wrongful act when I reprimanded my child														
Told my child it makes me angry when (behavior)														
I was accepting of some misbehaviors that were not serious														
Made my child converse by asking many questions														
Praised my child														
Spent at least 5–10 minutes alone with my child														

SECTION V

How to React When Your Child Intentionally Misbehaves

If your child does, or is doing, something wrong that you cannot tolerate or ignore and you are sure that your child knows the act is wrong, then punishment is warranted. If you are not sure that he knows the act is wrong, see Section IV. If the misbehavior occurs again after Section IV is utilized, punishment may be necessary. Punish your child in the same way each day for similar misbehaviors.

There are primarily two types of intentional misbehaviors:

A. Your child has already misbehaved; he has committed an act he knew was wrong before he did it.

B. Your child wishes to do something you cannot allow and cries and argues.

You should respond the following way to each situation:

A. Your Child Has Already Misbehaved and Needs to be Punished

Express your dissatisfaction. Tell him you are upset; be specific in your description of the misbehavior so you are sure your child knows what he has done wrong. Then send your child to his room for five minutes. Do not engage in lengthy and repeated explanations of the wrongful act and do not argue with your child. Calmly say to him "Mommy gets upset when you *(fill in misbehavior)* and cannot let you do this. You must go to your room for five minutes." If necessary, take his hand and lead him to his room. Ignore crying, temper tantrums, verbal denunciations, and disfluencies. Keep the door open. Ignore any negative behavior that follows. If he comes out of his room, add another minute to his time and tell him you will do so each time he leaves his room. If he continues to come out say, "Next time you come out I will close the door." Close the door if he continues to come out. If your child persists in asking when the time is up, use a kitchen timer with a bell. When you send your child to his room, try to remove or lock away all of his favorite toys. To be

49

effective punishment, being sent to his room should be as uninteresting a time as you can make it. (Your child should not have to go to bed if he is sent to his room.)

B. Your Child Wishes to Misbehave and Nags, Cries, Argues

Your child may wish to engage in activities that you cannot allow because they are dangerous, they conflict with your schedule, or they are excessive in nature. You owe your child an explanation why he cannot do what he wishes to do, but after you explain, do not engage in an argument. You also need to provide your child with verbal recognition that you realize he is upset. This lets him know you are not insensitive to the way he feels.

Say to him:

"I realize you are upset and want to *(fill in activity)."*

But

1. *Explain why he cannot do what he wishes* (i.e., too dark to go outside to play) and
2. Say "If you did this, it would upset me or make me angry."

After you have recognized that your child is upset, stated the reason he cannot do what he wishes, and explained that you would be angry if you let him do what he wants, ignore all his negative behaviors (i.e., nagging, crying, temper tantrums, verbal denunciations, or disfluency). If he continues to react negatively and you can no longer tolerate his behavior, leave the situation (i.e., take a walk or go to the next room).

If your child hits you or follows you, send him to his room.

Say to him:

"Mommy gets upset when you cry, nag, and argue for a long time. You must go to your room for five minutes." Ignore any negative behavior that follows. Add another minute if he walks out of his room and explain to him you will add time every time he leaves his room. If he still comes out, close the door.

C. Spanking

Spanking is seldom an advisable punishment and may cause bodily harm to your child. Spanking may stop a misbehavior but may also create distrust and fear of you. To be excluded from interaction with others, as is the case when a child goes to his room, is as effective as spanking but without the emotional overlay. However, there may be certain rare situations in which your child is in danger, such as running into the street, or when he is threatening danger to others, i.e., biting his baby sister. In these instances it may be necessary to respond quickly and forcefully, showing the utmost in disapproval. A fast spanking on his hand or rear is usually sufficient to convey your anger. Since you will not be using hitting regularly as a form of punishment, its use will have more significance to your child and define for him truly unacceptable behavior.

Section V—Questionnaire

Please complete this questionnaire and bring it with you to the next session.

Name ————————————————— Date—————————

1. What are the two types of intentional misbehaviors?
   1)——————————————————————————.
   2) ——————————————————————————.
2. If your child spilled his milk only one time, this would likely be:
   a) an intentional misbehavior
   b) an unintentional misbehavior
   c) both
3. If your child colored the mirror with crayons, then refused to help you clean the mirror, his misbehavior would be considered:
   a) intentional
   b) unintentional
   c) both
4. If your child has already misbehaved and needs to be punished, what would you do? (Check the appropriate behaviors.)
   a) Tell him you are upset.
   b) Spank him.
   c) Send him to his room for an hour.
   d) Engage in lengthy and repeated explanations.
   e) Send him to his room for five minutes.
   f) Send your child to his room even if he cries or throws a temper tantrum.
   g) Take his hand and lead him to his room if necessary.
   h) If he is disfluent, stop punishing him.
   i) Keep the door open.
   j) If he comes out of his room, let him go outside.
   k) If he comes out, add a minute to his time.
   l) If he kicks the wall while in his room, ignore this behavior.
   m) Use a kitchen timer with a bell to help him know when his time is up.

n) Have a lot of toys in his room so he won't be bored during the "time out" period.

o) If he continues to come out of his room, warn him—"Next time you come out, I will close the door."

p) He should go to bed if sent to his room.

q) When he misbehaves, tell him, "Mommy gets upset when you *(misbehavior)* and you must go to your room for five minutes."

r) If your child tries to argue with you about going to his room and he is disfluent, stop insisting that he go to his room.

5. If your child *wishes* to misbehave, you should take the following actions (check the ones you would do):

a) Tell your child that he is a "bad boy."

b) Tell him, "You cannot do this because I say so."

c) If necessary, argue with your child so he understands why he can't do what he wants.

d) Say to your child, "If you keep on arguing, I will not let you go out and play."

e) Say to him, "*I realize you're upset* and want to go outside but it's too dark to go outside." Other examples would be:

.....cut paper in the living room, but paper in the living room makes a mess."

.....take your sister's toy, but your sister has a right to play with her toys."

.....watch T.V., but it's time to go to bed and we must shut off the T.V."

.....play with your food, but playing with food is very messy and not good manners."

6. After you have explained the situation:

a) Answer any and all questions your child has.

b) Ignore any negative behavior like nagging.

c) If he cries and is disfluent, tell him you're sorry.

d) Spank him.

7. If your child cries for a long period of time and you cannot ignore it any longer, you should (select two):

a) Send him to his room.

b) Spank him.

c) Leave the room or go for a walk.

8. If your child hits you, hit him back.
   True_____ False_____

9. If your child is crying and nagging, tell him that his behavior upsets you before sending him to his room.
   True_____ False_____

10. You can spank your child if (select two):
    a) He is endangering his life.
    b) He tries to hurt his sister or brother.
    c) He hits you on the leg.
    d) He comes out of his room during the "time out" period.

Section V—Checklist

Name: _____   Date: _____

Write number of times each behavior occurred, a 0 if it did not occur, and an X if statement is irrelevant.

	Mon.	Tues.	Wed.	Thur.	Fri.	Sat.	Sun.
Punished my child the same way as yesterday for similar misbehaviors							
When I was angry, I told my child that I was and what made me displeased							
Sent my child to his room for five minutes							
Stopped punishing my child because he was disfluent							
Let my child know what he did wrong, then punished him							
Added a minute to my child's time spent in his room if he came out before I told him he could							
Ignored all negative behaviors (temper tantrums, crying, nagging) when sending my child to his room							
Explained the reason my child could not do what he wished							
Used the word "no"							
Told him to stop "stuttering"							

55

SECTION VI

Responding Consistently to Your Child's Misbehaviors

A. Establishing Daily Consistency

Parents should respond to their child's misbehaviors the same way every day, and an irritating act should not elicit your sharp reprimand and a "time out" period one day and a mild nod of disapproval the next. Consistency in your response to your child's action will help him know what pleases and displeases you. Punishing your child should not be dependent on whether *you* are having a good day. When you are ready to punish your child, *think*—"How did I handle a situation like this yesterday?" All misbehaviors, whether intentional or unintentional, should be handled the same way each day.

Construct the following chart and fill it in at the end of the day after your child is asleep. This chart will help you note how you responded today to your child's misbehaviors and if you responded today as you did yesterday or the day before.

Date	Child's misbehavior	How did I punish him today?	How have I punished him before?

B. Establishing Consistency between Parents

Both parents should sit down and discuss what constitutes a misbehavior and what is acceptable or at least a non-punishable act. Clearly, consistency cannot be obtained in the home if one parent disciplines the child while the other parent finds the child's actions permissable.

Both parents should discuss several examples of common misbehaviors and decide how they would treat them. For example: Does not go to bed. Spills milk. Hits sister. Does not eat vegetables. Breaks bottle. It is helpful to make a list of misbehaviors and write next to them how you will respond (see below). This not only allows each parent to be consistent with the other but also establishes day to day consistency in each parent's action. Bring this list to the next session so that you can discuss it with the clinician.

Misbehavior	Punishment That I Would Use	
	Mom	Dad

C. Disfluency Does not Alter Consistency

If in the course of misbehaving your child attempts to explain or clarify his situation and is disfluent, this (disfluency) does not alter your response to him. Consistency in the administration of punishment remains irregardless of your child's speech pattern.

D. Preparation of a List of Chores

Prepare a list of eight to ten chores you expect your child to do every day. Examples: Brushes teeth correctly. Takes a nice bath and dries himself. Is ready for school on time. Goes to bed and falls asleep.

You should also make another list of presents (i.e., toys, games, trips, cookies, and candy) that your child wants to have.

These two lists will be used in constructing the star chart, which will be explained to you at the next session.

Section VI—Questionnaire

Please complete this questionnaire and bring it with you to the next session.

Name _____ Date_____

1. In order to be consistent, what should you think about before you punish your child?

   _____

   _____.

2. By responding the same way each time a misbehavior occurs, you are establishing _____ in the way you manage your child.

3. If you send your child to his room on Monday for nagging, you should _____for nagging on Tuesday.

4. Not only should punishment be consistent from day to day, but also both parents should

   _____

   _____.

5. If you are about to punish your child and he is disfluent while trying to explain the situation or is arguing with you, you should:
   a) Not punish him.
   b) Tell him you do not care if he "stutters," the punishment stays.
   c) Ignore the disfluency and punish him.
   d) Spank him.

Section VI—Checklist

Name: _____

Date: _____

Write number of times each behavior occurred, a 0 if it did not occur, and an X if statement is irrelevant.

	Mon.	Tues.	Wed.	Thur.	Fri.	Sat.	Sun.
Punished my child the same as yesterday for similar misbehaviors							
Did not punish my child because he was disfluent							
Paid attention to what my child was saying							
Asked my child to recite a nursery rhyme							
Remained calm when my child misbehaved							
Referred only to the misbehavior when I reprimanded							
Presented a way my child could correct a misbehavior							
Accepted a misbehavior that was not serious, although it was irritating							
Sent my child to his room							
Spanked my child							
Spent time alone with my child							

SECTION VII

Constructing a Star Chart

A. Introduction

Adults usually work for a living, that is, they perform certain activities and are paid with money for these functions. The items they buy with this money act as one of the incentives to do work.

Not unlike the adult, the child has things that he wants. The little toy truck may be as important to him as a new car is to the adult. We can *buy* the car, but we probably will *give* our child the toy truck. We then ask or fight with our child to do certain activities or "chores" for free, or more ideologically because "he should be a good boy."

If your child does not see a definite relationship between what you ask him to do and what you give him, then this needs to be clarified. The purpose of the star chart is to set up a specific way of informing your child that when he does his chores he can obtain what he wants, but if he does not do what is expected he will have to do without.

B. Constructing a Star Chart

Construct a star chart that lists the chores you would like your child to do. Use script, drawings, or pictures to identify each activity. Everyday he should receive a star for each activity performed. The chart should be placed in his room or on the kitchen wall so he can watch the number of stars increase (Figure 1).

Make another chart listing the rewards your child will receive when he obtains a certain number of stars. Preferably, you should draw a picture of the item or clip a picture out of a magazine and paste it on the chart. When he sees a new toy he wants, add it to the chart (Figure 2).

C. Selecting the Behaviors for the Chart

Behaviors listed on the Star Chart should be described positively, not negatively. Try to avoid listing behaviors your child should not engage in; rather, select those activities or

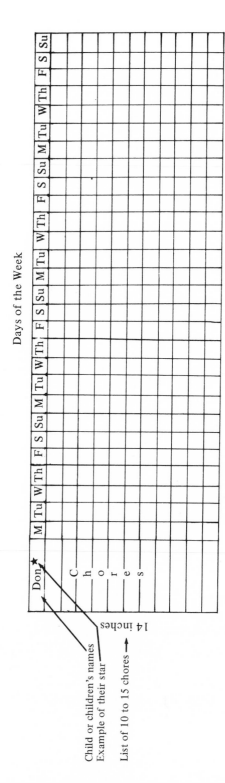

Figure 1. Star Chart

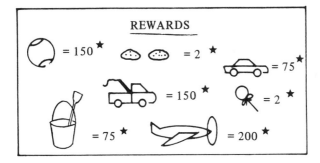

REWARDS

= 150 ★   = 2 ★   = 75 ★

= 150 ★   = 2 ★

= 75 ★   = 200 ★

Figure 2. Reward Chart

chores you would like him to do. For example, "Took a nice bath" is better than "Does not spill water on the floor." Explain to your child how to perform an activity correctly. This may necessitate telling him what not to do or why he will not receive a star if he does not do what is requested. The actual star should be reserved only for the reinforcement of positive behaviors. For example, you may have to explain to him that "Going to bed nicely" means promptly going into bed at 9:00 without arguments or "Behaves while driving in the car" means no yelling or jumping while Mommy is driving.

Examples of activities:
1. Takes turns when talking (see Section II)
2. Brushes teeth correctly
3. Dresses himself or cooperates while parents dress him
4. Stays near Mommy in the supermarket
5. Takes a bath nicely
6. Goes to bed and falls asleep
7. Makes his own bed
8. Is ready for school on time
9. Shares his toys with his sister

D. Star Chart for All Siblings

If there are other children in the family, between 3 and 11 years of age, these children should be included on the star chart. Each child should have a different color star and the child's name with his star should appear on the top of the chart.

E. Fighting Among Siblings

If, as in many homes, fighting among siblings is a problem, the chart can be used to reduce the conflict. This behavior should be listed on the star chart as "Plays nicely with his sister in the morning" or "Plays nicely with his sister before bedtime." Although you may have to tell your child that playing nicely means not hitting, the star chart should state the positive act of playing the correct way.

When stating this behavior, list several small blocks of time (i.e., morning, afternoon, before bedtime) in order to give your child a better opportunity to receive stars. He may not fight with his sibling in the morning, but may at night. A general statement such as "Played nicely with *(name)* today" would prevent your rewarding him for his good behavior in the morning.

F. Your Child Forgets To Do a Chore

If your child continually forgets a chore, you can remind him that he needs to do it in order to obtain a star. For example, if he usually forgets to brush his teeth before bedtime, a reminder while he is taking his bath may prevent your having to remind him later after he has forgotten to do the task. When you tell him not to forget to do a chore, always act as if you are his "partner" and want to help him acquire as many stars as he can. Therefore, when you remind him to do something you are just not "on him," but you are working with him to obtain stars.

Do not threaten your child by withholding stars if he does not do what he is asked. For example, it is wrong to say, "If you do not brush your teeth you will not get a star." It is much better to positively say, "When you brush your teeth you will receive a star, and I want you to get as many stars as you can." However, if he does not brush his teeth, of course he gets no stars and no rewards.

G. Judge the Difficulty of a Chore

Be careful not to make the tasks or chores too difficult for your child. He may need help in cleaning his room, so an item on the chart may read "Help Mommy clean up my room" instead of "Cleans up room."

H. Awarding Stars

Stars should be awarded as soon after the good behavior as possible. Do not wait until bedtime or the next day to paste the stars. Periodically praise your child about his star chart if he has accumulated a considerable number of stars.

I. "Cashing In" the Stars

When your child obtains a few stars, he earns a present (i.e., pieces of candy or cookies) or, especially with an older child, he can save the stars for something very special (i.e., a toy, a trip to the park or beach, money, or ice cream) (see Figure 2).

Some children may not need a tangible reward, since the stars are enough of an award for good behavior. Other children like to "earn" a present. Before introducing the star chart, decide how much each star is worth. Expensive presents or trips may be worth a hundred or more stars. Remember, stars can add up fast, so do not give presents away too cheaply. A guide you may use is to make each star worth 2¢, so that 50 stars are worth a dollar present.

As stars are used for presents, they should be marked off. *No present is given if there are not enough stars to earn it.* When there are an insufficient number of stars, you will have to tell your child he cannot have what he desires until he has enough stars. If he cries, has a temper tantrum, or is disfluent, ignore this behavior or send him to his room.

J. Stars for "Being Good"

If you find that your child is too young to understand the concept of specific stars for specific chores, you may wish to give stars for "being good" or doing what he was told. You will need to construct the star chart differently. Give one star for "being good" in the morning, one for the afternoon, and one for night. Draw a line on the chart at places where he can obtain a reward. For example:

Don ★	M	Tu	W	Th	F	S	Su	M	Tu	W	Th	F	S	Su	M	Tu	W
Morning																	
Afternoon																	
Night																	

K. Activities Worth More Stars

You may wish to make a difficult chore worth more stars. For example, if he continues to take his sister's toy, then the opposite activity "Plays nicely with his sister in the morning," may be worth two or even three stars. You can note on the star chart that an activity is worth more stars by placing two or three stars next to that activity. This way the child will be reminded that this item is particularly important.

Section VII—Questionnaire

Please complete this questionnaire and bring it to the next session.

Name _____ Date_____

1. Why do we need a star chart?

   _____
   _____
   _____.

2. If our boss at work told us what to do, but refused to pay us, we would_____.

3. The child has things that he wants and they may be as important to him as the car or house is to us.
   True_____ False_____

4. The star chart should include
   a)_____.
   b)_____.
   c) _____.

5. There should also be another chart that lists

   _____
   _____.

6. Which items are phrased the best for the star chart? (select two)
   a) Played nicely with his sister today.
   b) Did not complain about the food.
   c) Played nicely with his sister in the morning.
   d) Ate dinner nicely.

7. If your child is not doing one of the chores you have listed:
   a) Threaten him by saying "If you do not clean your room, you will not get a star."
   b) Act as his partner and remind him "When you clean your room, you get stars."

8. If he does not have enough stars for a present he wants and starts speaking disfluently:
   a) Give him the present.
   b) Tell him he will have to earn more stars.
   c) Give him several more stars although he hasn't earned them.

Section VII—Checklist

Name: _____

Date: _____

Write number of times each behavior occurred, a 0 if it did not occur, and an X if statement is irrelevant.

	Mon.	Tues.	Wed.	Thur.	Fri.	Sat.	Sun.
Threatened to withhold stars when my child did not do what he was asked							
Gave my child a star each time he did one of the items listed							
Told my child to speak more slowly							
Gave my child a present even if he did not have enough stars							
Gave my child stars if he cried or spoke disfluently							
Took turns to talk							
Spanked my child							
Had my child wait until I was through with what I was doing, then gave him my full attention							

APPENDICES

Appendix I:
Pre/Post Program Rating Scale

Name:_____ Date:_____

PRE/POST PROGRAM RATING SCALE

1. I spank my child when he speaks disfluently ("stutters")   Never___ Rarely___ Occasionally___ Frequently___ Always___

2. I tell my child to stop stuttering   Never___ Rarely___ Occasionally___ Frequently___ Always___

3. I help my child with a difficult word   Never___ Rarely___ Occasionally___ Frequently___ Always___

4. I tell my child to speak more slowly   Never___ Rarely___ Occasionally___ Frequently___ Always___

5. I give my child my immediate attention when he talks to me   Never___ Rarely___ Occasionally___ Frequently___ Always___

6. If my child has a temper tantrum, I give in to his demands   Never___ Rarely___ Occasionally___ Frequently___ Always___

7. If my child is disfluent, I give him my attention faster   Never___ Rarely___ Occasionally___ Frequently___ Always___

8. I tell others my child stutters   Never___ Rarely___ Occasionally___ Frequently___ Always___

9. If I am busy, and he wants my attention, I tell him he will have to wait until I am through   Never___ Rarely___ Occasionally___ Frequently___ Always___

10. Everyone has his turn to talk   Never___ Rarely___ Occasionally___ Frequently___ Always___

11. No one interrupts another person when he is talking   Never___ Rarely___ Occasionally___ Frequently___ Always___

71

12. I praise my child for things he does well

Never___ Rarely___ Occasionally___

Frequently___ Always___

13. I use the words "no," "can't," "stop it"

Never___ Rarely___ Occasionally___

Frequently___ Always___

14. I spend at least 5–10 minutes alone with my child each day

Never___ Rarely___ Occasionally___

Frequently___ Always___

15. I ask my child to tell me what he did today

Never___ Rarely___ Occasionally___

Frequently___ Always___

16. I tell my child to "stop stuttering"

Never___ Rarely___ Occasionally___

Frequently___ Always___

17. When my child misbehaves, I tell him he is a "bad boy"

Never___ Rarely___ Occasionally___

Frequently___ Always___

18. When my child misbehaves, I want to know "why"

Never___ Rarely___ Occasionally___

Frequently___ Always___

19. I give my child a way he can correct his misbehavior

Never___ Rarely___ Occasionally___

Frequently___ Always___

20. To show my interest, I ask my child a lot of questions

Never___ Rarely___ Occasionally___

Frequently___ Always___

21. I punish my child the same way every day

Never___ Rarely___ Occasionally___

Frequently___ Always___

22. I spank my child when he irritates me

Never___ Rarely___ Occasionally___

Frequently___ Always___

23. I tell my child to speak more slowly when he is having trouble

Never___ Rarely___ Occasionally___

Frequently___ Always___

24. When my child misbehaves, I send him to his room

Never___ Rarely___ Occasionally___

Frequently___ Always___

25. When I punish my child, I let him know what he did wrong

Never___ Rarely___ Occasionally___

Frequently___ Always___

26. When my child is disfluent, I do not punish him

Never___ Rarely___ Occasionally___

Frequently___ Always___

27. My husband (wife) uses the same punishment that I do

Never___ Rarely___ Occasionally___

Frequently___ Always___

28. I spend time alone with my child

Never___ Rarely___ Occasionally___

Frequently___ Always___

29. I give my child a reward when he does his chores

Never___ Rarely___ Occasionally___

Frequently___ Always___

30. If my child spills or breaks something, I spank him

Never___ Rarely___ Occasionally___

Frequently___ Always___

31. My child repeats the first sounds or syllables of words two or more times

Never___ Rarely___ Occasionally___

Frequently___ Always___

32. My child holds out a sound in a word for over a second

Never___ Rarely___ Occasionally___

Frequently___ Always___

33. My child speaks with effort or tension

Never___ Rarely___ Occasionally___

Frequently___ Always___

34. My child uses "uh" while he is talking

Never___ Rarely___ Occasionally___

Frequently___ Always___

35. My child seems to be concerned about his speech

Never___ Rarely___ Occasionally___

Frequently___ Always___

36. My child is disfluent (has speaking difficulty)

Never___ Rarely___ Occasionally___

Frequently___ Always___

Appendix II:
Questionnaire Answers

SECTION I

1. 1) Tell him "I will listen to you after I am finished."
    2) Find a convenient stopping place in my activity so that I do not keep him waiting long.
2. When my child is disfluent, I should give him the *same* amount of attention that I do when he is fluent.
3. I will not:
    1) Hit him.
    2) Tell him to "stop stuttering."
    3) Threaten punishment for "poor" speech.
    4) Help him with the word.
    5) Tell him to speak more slowly.
    6) Tell him to think about what he's going to say.
4. No
5. I should explain to him that I want to know what he has to say, but first I must finish what I am doing before I can listen to him.
6. a
    c
7. 1) Remain calm and act as though he were speaking fluently.
    2) Pay attention to *what* he is saying.
    3) Show him that I enjoy talking to him and am interested in what he has to say.

SECTION II

1. False
2. Talking about future events is likely to be easier for my child.
3. Take turns
4. False
5. c
6. Past
7. Stuttering is an abnormal speech pattern that is often characterized by uneven repetitions, long hesitations, silent blocks, and facial grimaces. The individual is conscious of his speech. This awareness may affect his verbal interactions with others.
8. No
9. b
10. Stop him, tell him that it is someone else's turn, and that he will have time to talk again after other people have spoken.
11. False

SECTION III

1. b
2. True

3. 5–10 minutes
4. b
5. Praise him.
6. 1) The word loses significance.
    2) This response becomes frustrating, punishing, and hurting.
7. False
8. "Did you have a good day?"
    "Did you like nursery school today?"
9. 2

SECTION IV

1. a, b, d, f, h
2. a

SECTION V

1. 1) My child commits an act he knew was wrong before he did it.
    2) My child cries and argues when I cannot allow him to do what
        he wishes.
2. b
3. a
4. a, e, f, g, i, k, l, m, o, q
5. e
6. b
7. a, c
8. False
9. True
10. a, b

SECTION VI

1. "How did I handle this situation yesterday?"
2. Consistency
3. Send him to his room.
4. Agree upon what constitutes a misbehavior and what is acceptable
    behavior.
5. c

SECTION VII

1. To help my child see a definite relationship between what I ask him
    to do and what I give him; or to set up a specific way of letting my
    child know that when he does his chores, he can obtain what he
    wants.
2. Stop working.
3. True

4. a) the name of my child
    b) list of specific daily chores
    c) days of the week
5. The rewards and the number of stars needed to obtain them.
6. c, d
7. b
8. b

References

Allen, K., and Harris, R. 1971. Eliminating a child's excessive scratching by training the mother in reinforcement procedures. In: A. Graziano (ed.), Behavior Therapy with Children. Chicago: Aldine Publishing Company.

Barbara, D. 1954. Stuttering: A Psychodynamic Approach to Its Understanding and Treatment. New York: Julian Press Inc.

Becker, W. 1971. Parents are Teachers: A Child Management Program. Champaign, Ill.: Research Press Company.

Blaunstein, P., and Wahler, R. 1971. Behavior modification: An attempt to influence childhood stuttering. J. TN Speech Hear. Assoc. 17:45–54.

Bloodstein, O. 1960. Development of stuttering. J. Speech Hear. Disord. 25:219–37.

Bloodstein, O. 1975a. Stuttering, tension and fragmentation. In: J. Eisenson (ed.), Stuttering: A Second Symposium. New York: Harper & Row.

Bloodstein, O. 1975b. A Handbook on Stuttering. Chicago: The National Easter Seal Society for Crippled Children and Adults.

Bluemel, C. 1932. Primary and secondary stammering, Quart. J. Speech 18: 187–200.

Brutten, E., and Shoemaker, D. 1967. The Modification of Stuttering. Englewood Cliffs, N.J.: Prentice-Hall Inc.

Christopherson, E., Arnold, C., Hill, D., and Quilitch, H. 1972. The home point system: Token reinforcement procedures for application by parents of children with behavior problems. J. Appl. Behav. Anal. 5:485–497.

Cohen, H. 1970. The P.I.C.A. project. Year Two. Project Interim Report. Programming Interpersonal Curricula for Adolescents. Silver Springs, Md.: Institute for Behavioral Research.

Davis, D. 1939, 1940. The relation of repetition in the speech of young children to certain measures of language maturation and situational factors. J. Speech Hear. Disord. 4:303–318; 5:242–246.

Egland, G. 1955. Repetitions and prolongations in the speech of stuttering and non-stuttering children. In: W. Johnson (ed.), Stuttering in Children and Adults. Minneapolis: University of Minnesota Press.

Emerick, L., and Hatten, J. 1974. Diagnosis and Evaluation in Speech Pathology. Englewood Cliffs, N.J.: Prentice-Hall Inc.

Glasner, P. 1947. Nature and treatment of stuttering. Am. J. Dis. Child. 74:218–25.

Gray, B., and England, G. 1969. Stuttering and the Conditioning Therapies. Monterey, Ca.: The Monterey Institute for Speech and Hearing.

Hall, R. 1974. Managing Behavior. Lawrence, Kansas: H and H Enterprises.

Hawkins, R., Peterson, R., Schweid, E., and Bijou, S. 1966. Behavior therapy in the home: Amelioration of problem parent-child relations with the parent in a therapeutic role. J. Exp. Child Psychol. 4:99–107.

Herbert, E., and Baer, D. 1972. Training parents as behavior modifiers: Self-recording of contingent attention. J. Appl. Behav. Anal. 5:139–149.

Johnson, P. 1951. An exploratory study of certain aspects of the speech histories of 23 former stutterers. Unpublished M.A. Thesis, University of Pittsburgh, Pittsburgh.

Johnson, W. 1942. A study of the onset and development of stuttering. J. Speech Disord. 7:251–257.

Johnson, W. 1949. An open letter to the mother of a stuttering child. J. Speech Hear. Disord. 14:3–8.

Johnson, W. 1959. The Onset of Stuttering. Minneapolis: University of Minnesota Press.

Lindsley, O. 1966. An experiment with parents handling behavior at home. Johnstone Bull. 9:27–36.

Luper, H., and Mulder, R. 1965. Stuttering Therapy for Children. Englewood Cliffs, N.J.: Prentice-Hall Inc.

O'Dell, S. 1974. Training parents in behavior modification: A review. Psychol. Bull. 81:418–433.

Patterson, G. 1965. A learning theory approach to the treatment of the school phobic child. In: L. Ullman and L. Krasner (eds.), Case Studies in Behavior Modification. New York: Holt, Rinehart, and Winston.

Patterson, G., and Gullion, M. 1968. Living with Children: New Methods for Parents and Teachers. Champaign, Ill.: Research Press Company.

Shames, G., and Sherrick, C. 1963. A discussion of nonfluency and stuttering as an operant behavior. J. Speech Hear. Disord. 28:3–18.

Shames, G., and Egolf, D. 1976. Operant Conditioning and the Management of Stuttering: A Book for Clinicians. Englewood Cliffs, N.J.: Prentice-Hall Inc.

Sheehan, J. 1975. Conflict theory and avoidance—reduction therapy. In: J. Eisenson (ed.), Stuttering: A Second Symposium. New York: Harper & Row.

Smith, J., and Smith, D. 1968. Child Management: A Program for Parents. Ann Arbor, Mich.: Ann Arbor Publishers.

Van Riper, C. 1963. Speech Correction: Principles and Methods. Englewood Cliffs, N.J.: Prentice-Hall Inc.

Van Riper, C. 1971. The Nature of Stuttering. Englewood Cliffs, N.J.: Prentice-Hall Inc.

Van Riper, C. 1973. The Treatment of Stuttering. Englewood Cliffs, N.J.: Prentice-Hall Inc.

Wahler, R., Winkel, G., Peterson, R., and Morrison, D. 1965. Mothers as behavior therapists for their own children. Behav. Res. Ther. 3:113–124.

Wingate, M. 1976. Stuttering: Theory and Treatment. New York: Irvington Publishers.

Wischner, G. 1950. Stuttering behavior and learning. J. Speech Hear. Disord. 15:324–335.

Young, M. 1961. Predicting ratings of severity of stuttering. J. Speech Hear. Disord. (Monogr. Suppl.) 7:31–54.

Zaleski, T. 1965. Rhythmic Skills in Stuttering Children. De Therapia Vocis et Loquellae 1:371–372.

Zeilberger, J., Sampen, S. E., and Sloane, H. N., Jr. 1968. Modification of a child's problem behaviors in the home with the mother as therapist. J. Appl. Behav. Anal. 1:47–53.

NOTES

NOTES

NOTES

NOTES

NOTES

NOTES